Pug is a pup.
Pug and Gus have fun in the sun.

2

Gus and Pug will run.
Will Gus win?

Gus and Pug run up the hill.
Run, Gus! Run, Pug!

3

4

Gus huffs! Gus puffs!
Pug huffs! Pug puffs!

Gus and Pug have a bun.
Yum! Yum! Yum!

5

6

Pug is in the tub.
Gus rubs Pug's suds.

Gus hugs Pug.
Gus and Pug are pals.

7

8   The pals nap on the rug.
Gus and Pug had fun in the sun.